CRISIS IN HAITI

Meish Goldish

THE MILLBROOK PRESS

Brookfield, Connecticut

Published by The Millbrook Press, Inc.
2 Old New Milford Road
Brookfield, CT 06804
© 1994 Blackbirch Graphics, Inc.

5 4 3 2 1

Created and produced in association with Blackbirch Graphics.
Series Editor: Tanya Lee Stone

Library of Congress Cataloging-in-Publication Data
Goldish, Meish.
    Crisis in Haiti / Meish Goldish.
        p.   cm. — (Headliners)
    Includes bibliographical references and index.
    ISBN 1-56294-553-X
    1. Haiti—Politics and government—1986—Juvenile literature. 2. Haiti—
Economic conditions—Juvenile literature. 3. Haiti—Social conditions—
Juvenile literature. [1. Haiti—Politics and government—1986. 2. Haiti—
Economic conditions. 3. Haiti—Social conditions.] I. Title. II. Series
F1928.2.G65   1995
972.9407'3—dc20
                                                                94-36052
                                                                CIP
                                                                AC

Contents

Chapter 1

A Nation Adrift

In mid-July 1994, the American battleship U.S.S. *Mount Whitney* sailed south from the United States to waters off the coast of Haiti. It joined thirteen other American warships that had already been sent to the area. Aboard the vessels were 2,400 U.S. Marines. They stood prepared to invade the Haitian shore if so ordered by the president of the United States, Bill Clinton. The *Mount Whitney*, loaded with communications gear, would serve as a floating headquarters in the event that an invasion of Haiti took place.

At the same time, dozens of other boats traveled away from Haiti. But these were not giant battleships with armed soldiers and sophisticated equipment. They were small, flimsy sailboats carrying Haitians who had only the clothes on their backs.

The sailboats, ironically, were headed north toward the United States. The passengers were Haitian refugees—people fleeing their homeland and seeking asylum (refuge, or safety) in America.

Since mid-June 1994, some 20,000 Haitians had risked the dangerous voyage to Florida. Most of them met with disappointment; some met with tragedy.

As conditions in Haiti worsen, a desperate nation searches for a solution.

Opposite:
Thousands of Haitians risked their lives attempting to sail to the United States. Here, a Coast Guard boat rescues sixty Haitians packed aboard a twenty-foot sailboat.

President Clinton had ordered the U.S. Coast Guard to stop any Haitian boats headed toward the United States. Thousands of refugees were intercepted at sea by Coast Guard officials. Most were taken to the American naval base at Guantánamo Bay, Cuba. Many other refugees, however, failed to make it even as far as a Coast Guard interception. Hundreds either drowned or died of starvation during their difficult journey north.

Why were the Haitian people so desperately trying to escape their homeland? And why was the United States poised for a possible invasion of their country? Answers to these questions lie in the turmoil that has long plagued the nation of Haiti.

Political Upheaval

Haiti is a country in the West Indies, about 600 miles southeast of Florida. It shares the island of Hispaniola with its neighbor, the Dominican Republic. Haiti has a long history of political instability. Although Haiti's constitution guarantees democracy and free elections, these rights have never been fully enforced by the government. For nearly its entire existence as a nation, Haiti has been not a democracy but a dictatorship. In this form of rule, the people of a nation are under the absolute authority of the government.

In 1985, after living with dictatorships for more than four decades, many Haitians began working to establish a democratic society. In December 1990, Haiti held its first-ever democratic elections. Father Jean-Bertrand Aristide, a liberal Roman Catholic priest, won the presidency by a landslide vote.

But true to trends in Haitian history, the new president did not remain in power for long. In September 1991, just seven months after his term began, President Aristide was ousted from office in a military coup, or violent overthrow. It was led by Lieutenant General Raoul Cédras, the commander of the Haitian army. Cédras seized control primarily because he objected to the president's programs, which included plans to reduce the power of the military.

The forced removal of President Aristide set off a bloody civil war in Haiti. The nation's poor demanded that Aristide be restored to office. But their vocal protests were no match for the Haitian military's guns. Aristide supporters began to be arrested, beaten, tortured, and killed. The attacks were carried out by three groups of Cédras enforcers—army soldiers, police officers, and civilians hired by the military. Haitians who attended

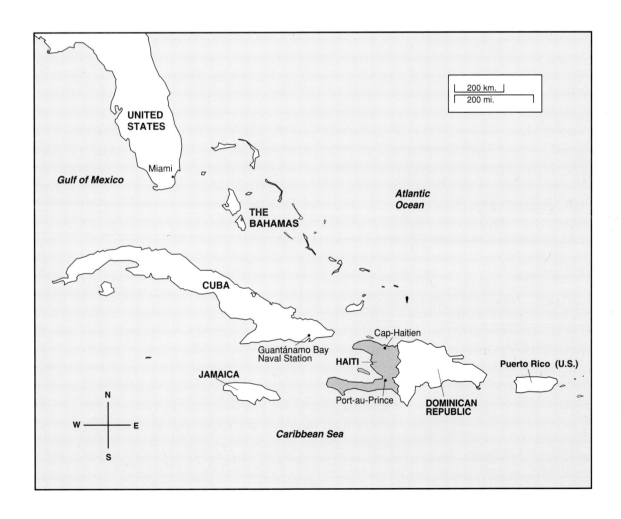

pro-democracy rallies, distributed political leaflets, or merely told neighbors that they favored Aristide's return risked death. In poor Haitian villages, young men regularly were shot at; young women frequently were raped.

As a result of the terror, waves of Haitians fled their homes to either hide elsewhere on the island or to sail to freedom in other countries. Thousands of refugees headed for America in rickety boats.

The U.S. government could not ignore this crisis in Haiti. Streams of Haitian refugees were sailing steadily toward Florida's shores. There were widespread reports

In May 1994, mourners attended a funeral for three men who were killed simply because they were supporters of Aristide.

Creole: The Language of the People

French and Creole are the official languages of Haiti. Yet nine out of ten Haitians cannot understand, speak, or write French. French is used only by the country's upper classes and government officials.

The majority of Haitians speak Creole. Creole is a blend of many languages that were spoken by different peoples who came to the island beginning in the late 1400s. Haitian Creole is a unique mixture of Spanish, French, English, Indian, and African languages. An example of the African influence on the Creole language can be heard in the absence of "r" or "s" sounds. The word Creole itself is pronounced "Cweole" by Haitians.

For centuries, Creole was only a spoken language in Haiti, not a written one. Then, in 1948, the United Nations sponsored a program to develop Creole as a written language. Scholars created official rules for spelling and grammar. They generally spelled words as they sounded, instead of how they were originally written in one of the source languages. For example, the Creole word for *master* comes from the French word *maître*, which is pronounced "met" in French. Therefore, the Creole word is spelled simply *met*.

The language of Creole is known for proverbs that reflect Haitian culture and philosophy. In describing the land of Haiti, Haitian's will say *Deye mon ge mon*, which means "Beyond the mountains, there are more mountains." One Haitian saying is *Che go kat pat, se you sel cheme li te*: "A dog has four paws, but it can only go one way." A proverb that reflects the Haitian devotion to religion is *Ka poul bwe dlo, li pa blie Bo-Die*, meaning "When a chicken drinks water, it doesn't forget to raise its head in thanks to God."

Perhaps the Haitian people's long distrust of government rulers is best reflected by this ancient Haitian proverb: *Se le koulev mouri, ou konn longe li.* "Only when the serpent dies can you measure it."

---

of terrible human rights abuses in Haiti. Over a three-year period, first President George Bush, then President Bill Clinton worked unsuccessfully to have President Aristide restored to power. By July 1994, Clinton was considering an American invasion of Haiti in order to remove Cédras from power.

An Ailing Economy

Even without political crises, Haiti has many serious problems. Haiti is one of the poorest countries in the Western Hemisphere. Most of the people suffer from terrible poverty, hunger, malnutrition, disease, illiteracy, and unemployment. The life expectancy of the average Haitian is only fifty-six years. One out of every eight babies in Haiti dies before reaching one year of age. Throughout the country there are children with orange hair, one symptom of malnutrition.

A Haitian boy searches for something to salvage in this open-air cooking facility in Port-au-Prince. In the early 1990s, economic sanctions caused an increase in poverty.

There are many reasons why Haiti is such a poor country. About three fourths of its workers are farmers. But because Haiti is largely rugged mountain terrain, workable farmland is scarce. Most farmers own less than two acres apiece, barely enough land on which to grow food for their families. They work with crude tools—pointed sticks and shovels. The soil is generally overworked and eroded. Most Haitians are too poor to buy the fertilizers that could enrich their worn-out land.

Haiti's ability to produce more crops is also affected by its climate. The country has two rainy seasons, one from April to June and another from October to November. But the rain often comes in heavy downpours that can flood land, ruin vegetation, and even drown people. In addition, seasonal hurricanes have been known to destroy Haitian crops.

Haiti also has very few industries. Coffee and sugarcane are the main exportable food products. Land erosion, the cutting down of trees for fuel, and tree diseases have destroyed much of the island nation's timber. Bauxite, an ore from which aluminum is made, is Haiti's only commercially mined substance. However, much of this natural resource has already been depleted. The country lacks the technology and money to develop its other natural resources—oil, copper, gold, silver, and coal. Because of Haiti's unstable political history, foreign companies have been unwilling to invest much money in the country.

Another largely undeveloped industry is commercial fishing. Although Haiti lies directly in the path of major fish migrations, Haitian fishermen seldom travel more than a few miles from their home ports. They lack both the modern equipment and reliable boats that are needed to do so.

Because of Haiti's weak economy, some 6 million of Haiti's approximately 6.5 million people live in slums throughout the country. Water that is safe to drink is scarce. In the capital city of Port-au-Prince, about 700,000 residents have no running water, no electricity, no sewage system, and no garbage removal. The living conditions are among the worst in the world. In rural areas, many Haitian families dwell in one-room huts. The walls are boards covered with clay and mud, and the roofs are made of straw or palm leaves. Most huts have no indoor plumbing or electricity.

The majority of Haiti's workers earn only about $370 a year. But not everyone in Haiti is poor. There is a small, but thriving, upper class. Approximately 1 percent of the population accumulates 50 percent of the national income. This huge difference in wealth is one of the main reasons for the turmoil in Haiti.

The nation of Haiti has the worst living conditions in the Western Hemisphere. Here, a boy tries to clean up an open sewer by using a fishing line to remove garbage.

Social Conflict

Haiti's political and economic problems are rooted in the division of its social classes. The majority of Haitians—about 95 percent—descend directly from black Africans who were brought to Haiti as slaves. Thus, Haiti has earned the nickname "Daughter of Africa." Today, most Haitians still follow the ancient customs of their African ancestors. These customs are reflected in Haitian art and music, the language of Creole, and the religious practice of *voodoo*.

About 5 percent of the Haitian population are either whites or *mulattos*. Mulattos are light-skinned people who have mixed black and white ancestry. Most of Haiti's mulattos belong to the middle and upper classes. They are frequently educated in France. Besides Creole, most mulattos also speak French. They live in modern houses, many in the mountains of Port-au-Prince. They prosper as business people, doctors, and lawyers.

The wide gap between the rich and poor in Haiti has created virtually two separate "countries." Generally, the whites and mulattos live very comfortable and privileged

Due to lack of funds for education, only a small percentage of Haitian children are able to attend school. In the small village of Dedume, sixty miles away from the city of Port-au-Prince, these students are fortunate to have a school in their community.

Voodoo: An Unofficial Religion

The official religion of Haiti is Roman Catholicism, which 75 percent of the people practice—to some extent. Yet many Haitians also practice voodoo (or *vodun*), a religion that blends ancient African and Christian beliefs. The term voodoo comes from a West African word meaning "god," "spirit," or "sacred object."

Followers of voodoo, called *voodooists*, believe that the world is filled with gods, demons, saints, and the spirits of ancestors. In voodoo tradition, there are many *loas*, or gods. These include the loas of farming, rain, love, war, and the sea.

Voodooists believe that by performing special ceremonies, they can become possessed by the loas and can then communicate with them. In a typical ceremony, a *houngan*, or voodoo priest, leads songs and prayers. Worshipers then dance to a loud drumbeat until they fall to the floor, exhausted. This is a sign that a loa has entered a worshiper's body and soul.

In Haiti, voodoo is also practiced as a means of medical treatment. Houngans practice healing with herbal medicines. Haiti has about one doctor for every 8,000 people, so the houngan is an important member of society. If a disease cannot be cured, the houngan explains it in terms of faith: The illness may have been sent by spirits of ancestors who are being neglected by their living descendants.

Voodooists are extremely careful to protect themselves from peril. For example, noon—when people generally cast no shadows—is considered to be a very dangerous time of day. Voodooists believe that when a shadow disappears, a person's soul has left the body. Without a soul, the person could be attacked by evil spirits. Voodooists will often wear special charms and cast spells to protect themselves from evil. The charms—they believe—can avert illness, keep enemies away, and bring love.

---

lives. But among the black masses, poverty and illiteracy reign. Although education is free (but many schools do charge for tuition, books, and uniforms) and required for children six to twelve years of age, there is a serious shortage of schools. Only about 20 percent of school-age children attend classes. And, only about 53 percent of Haiti's entire population can read and write.

Historically, Haiti's poor and uneducated blacks have received little attention from government rulers. The elite white and mulatto minority have held most of the political influence. The 1990 election of President Aristide was significant because it brought the potential for widespread change. It held the promise for a democratic society and help for Haiti's poor. The military coup in 1991, however, reminded Haitians of how difficult it is to bring real change to their country.

The problems that plague Haiti are not simple. To fully appreciate their complexity, one must look at Haiti's past to see how it affects both its present and its future.

Chapter 2

A History of Revolution

T he troubles that plague Haiti today have a long and bitter history dating back more than 500 years. The Arawak Indians, the indigenous (native) people who lived on the island at that time, called their home *Hayti*, meaning "Land of Mountains." When Christopher Columbus arrived, he renamed the land *La Isla Española* ("The Spanish Island"). The name was later shortened to *Hispaniola*. This was just the first of many changes that the Europeans would come to impose on the native people of this area.

> For hundreds of years, revolutions and military coups have been a way of life in Haiti.

The Arrival of Columbus

On December 8, 1492, Columbus and his crew landed at what is now the Haitian city of Cap-Haitien. There they encountered the Arawak Indians, who had lived on the island for hundreds of years. Leaving some men behind, Columbus left to explore more of the Caribbean. He then went home to Spain. Returning to Hispaniola a year later, he found all of his men dead. Some historians believe that the Arawak Indians murdered them; others believe that another tribe, the Caribs from South America, was responsible for their deaths.

Opposite:
In 1492, Christopher Columbus was the first white person to set foot on the island of Hispaniola. Upon arrival, he met the Arawak Indians who were native to the island.

Despite this setback, thousands more Spanish settlers traveled to Hispaniola. Over the next twenty years, the Spanish established many villages. The settlers forced the Indians to mine gold and grow food for them. If they resisted, the Spanish killed them. By 1840, the Arawak people no longer existed—they had become extinct. The Arawaks died of both cruel treatment and of new diseases brought by the settlers. However, the Spanish still desired slave laborers, so they imported African slaves.

A Thriving French Colony

During the mid-1500s, most Spanish settlers left Hispaniola for richer settlements in Peru and Mexico. French pirates seized part of the abandoned island, and Spain was unable to stop them. In 1697, Spain officially gave the western third of Hispaniola to France, which then renamed the territory St. Domingue. That is the area known today as Haiti. The Spanish kept control of the eastern two thirds of the island, which is now the Dominican Republic.

In St. Domingue, French colonists built huge sugarcane and coffee plantations. They also grew tobacco and cotton. During the 1700s, St. Domingue became the richest European colony in the Western Hemisphere. By 1790, it was producing 40 percent of the world's sugar and 50 percent of the world's coffee.

But French colonists could not accomplish all this by themselves. They relied heavily on black slave labor, just as the Spanish had done earlier. The French imported African slaves in huge volume. By 1790, there were half a million slaves in St. Domingue—eight times as many black slaves as white colonists!

French masters forced the slaves to toil long hours in the fields. Workers never had time off. For their labor, they received little food and clothing and only tiny huts in which to live.

In 1791, the slaves rebelled. They killed thousands of white colonists and burned crops, fields, and plantations. Unable to control the rebellion, France declared the slaves free in 1794. But fighting continued as both Spanish and British invaders tried to capture the land amidst the chaos. Black rebels also battled mulattos, who had become land and slave owners over the years.

Toussaint L'Ouverture, a former slave, managed to take control of the government. He restored order in St. Domingue until 1799, when France's emperor Napoleon Bonaparte sent the French army to retake the colony.

The 1791 rebellion was successful in forcing the French to free all black slaves by 1794.

A Haitian Hero: Toussaint L'Ouverture

Toussaint L'Ouverture was a major force in liberating St. Domingue from foreign rule.

There is one man who many believe symbolizes Haiti's struggle for freedom more than any other single person. Born François Dominique Toussaint in 1743, to parents who were black slaves, Toussaint was a slave himself until he was forty-nine. However, he had a sympathetic master, who taught him how to read and write.

When the slaves of St. Domingue rebelled against their French rulers in 1791, Toussaint led a troop of 4,000 rebels. Toussaint's army, along with other slave forces, battled the French until 1794, when France freed its slaves. But even after this victory, the fighting continued. This time Toussaint fought the Spanish and English, who sought to control the island in the midst of the chaos. Toussaint feared that if Spain and England were victorious, they might bring back slavery to the colony.

Finally, the Spanish withdrew from St. Domingue in 1795. By then, Toussaint had been given a new name—L'Ouverture—which means "The Opening." This name came from a remark that St. Domingue's governor made about Toussaint: "This man finds an opening everywhere," meaning that Toussaint had the remarkable ability to easily break through any enemy lines.

Toussaint's efforts had caused the French to free the slaves and the Spanish to withdraw. But his battles in St. Domingue were not yet over. In 1799, a civil war broke out between the island's blacks and mulattos. Toussaint led black fighters against the forces of General André Rigaud, who wanted the island to be under mulatto control. Toussaint defeated Rigaud in 1800. More than 10,000 mulattos died in the fighting.

Toussaint now controlled the country. But a challenge lay ahead. The nation had been destroyed by war. The economy was ruined, and the people were weary. Toussaint began to repair and rebuild. As governor of St. Domingue, he ordered the killing of mulattos to stop. He also convinced many white plantation owners to return to the colony to help rebuild it. Toussaint expelled the Spanish from the eastern part of the island in 1801, and freed the slaves still living there.

Toussaint wrote a new constitution for the people of St. Domingue. It declared that workers would be guaranteed modest wages, housing, and medical care. Toussaint also named himself dictator for life.

Not surprisingly, the French, who once controlled the colony and still lived there, were not happy with Toussaint's new constitution. Their ruler, Napoleon Bonaparte, felt that Toussaint's self-appointment as dictator for life was an insult. Toussaint was captured by French troops and sent to prison in France, where he died in 1803.

Toussaint L'Ouverture has never been forgotten by his people. Today, Haitians remember him as a hero who helped bring an end to slavery in Haiti.

Toussaint was later captured and imprisoned in France, where he died. But the French were not victorious. Many soldiers caught yellow fever and died. Greatly weakened, France finally surrendered the island in 1803.

An Independent Nation

On January 1, 1804, General Jean-Jacques Dessalines, a leader of the black rebels named by Toussaint during his reign, declared St. Domingue an independent country. He renamed it the Republic of Haiti. Haiti became the second free nation in the Western Hemisphere (the first was the United States). It also became the first black-led republic in the world.

Dessalines appointed himself Haiti's emperor. But he faced many serious problems, both internal and external. Years of fighting had destroyed the economy. Furthermore, other nations refused to recognize Haiti because its leadership was black. In the United States, slave owners in the South were especially fearful. If blacks could rebel in Haiti, they worried, would they also rebel in America?

Under the rule of Dessalines, Haiti became the first black-led republic in the world.

Ironically, Dessalines became a cruel ruler. Unsympathetic to former slave owners, at one point he ordered his army to kill all whites. His harshness offended many of his supporters. Unable to lead the country to economic recovery, Dessalines was assassinated in 1806.

After Dessalines's death, Haiti became politically divided. In 1808, the nation was sectioned in half, each half with its own president. In the north, former slave Henri Christophe ruled the blacks. In the south, Alexandre Pétion ruled the mulattos. A decade later, the country was finally reunited, but struggles between blacks and mulattos continued for many years.

Jean-Pierre Boyer, a mulatto, served as president from 1818 to 1843. His twenty-five years in office represent the longest period that any single person has ever ruled in Haiti. From 1844 to 1914, no fewer than thirty-two different men headed the unstable government.

During Boyer's rule, Haitians gained control of the eastern two thirds of Hispaniola, the Dominican Republic. Dominicans did not regain their land until Boyer's rule ended. Because of this long takeover, bitter resentments between Haitians and Dominicans remain to this day.

The U.S. Occupation of Haiti

Almost sixty years after Haiti became a republic, in 1862, President Abraham Lincoln granted Haiti official diplomatic recognition—an important political gesture to the black nation. This marked the beginning of U.S. involvement in Haiti. Fifty-one years later, the United States became much more seriously involved.

Between 1911 and 1915, a passage of only four years, a total of six Haitian presidents were overthrown or murdered by Haitians who were angry about the poverty in their country. After a Haitian crowd killed Vilbrun Guillaume Sam, the sixth presidential victim, President Woodrow Wilson of the United States decided to act.

In 1915, President Wilson ordered 2,000 U.S. Marines into Haiti. He feared that Germany might otherwise try to capture the unstable island as a base from which to attack the United States. He also wanted to guarantee that Haiti would keep up its payments on a $21.5 million debt to the U.S. government.

Many Haitians bitterly resented the American occupation of their country. They saw it as a return to the days of white rule. About 20,000 Haitians revolted. It took the Haitian police and the U.S. Marines more than two years to bring the fighting to an end. More than 2,000 Haitian rebels died in the uprising.

In July 1915, U.S. Marines boarded a ship in Philadelphia, bound for Haiti. The marines remained on the island for nineteen years.

Haitians: A People Divided

For centuries, bitter conflict has existed between Haiti's black and mulatto populations. The blacks are descendants of African slaves who were imported by the European settlers beginning in the early 1500s. The mulattos are light-skinned people who have both black and white ancestors.

Traditionally in Haiti, mulattos have enjoyed a higher social standing than blacks. In the 1780s, the mulattos, known in French as *gens de couleur* ("people of color"), ranked second in power. Whites ranked first—they owned about two thirds of the slaves and farmland in the colony. Mulattos owned the remaining third. What they desired was to have equality with whites on the island. Their attitude of superiority fostered resentment among blacks.

Hatred between Haiti's blacks and mulattos did not end with the slave rebellion of the 1790s. For the next 150 years, the groups continued to fight over control of the leadership of Haiti. Not until 1946, during the "Black Revolution," was significant change for blacks established in the country. That year, Dumarsais Estimé became the first black since 1915 to serve as Haitian president. His election marked a temporary end to mulatto dominance in Haiti. He wrote a new constitution that reflected the will of the Haitian black majority.

After hundreds of years of struggle, Haitian blacks and mulattos are still at odds today. Only time will tell if the economic imbalances and racial resentments that divide the two groups will ever be erased.

Despite resistance, the United States tried to improve conditions in Haiti. It even helped Haiti to pay off the republic's huge debts to other nations. The United States also funded projects that built highways, hospitals, and schools in Haiti. And it helped to write a democratic constitution for the republic. In 1934, after nineteen years of occupation, U.S. Marines finally left Haiti.

Military Rule

Although Haitians regained self-rule when the U.S. occupation ended, they were still unable to achieve peace. In 1937, Haiti found itself at war with its island neighbor, the Dominican Republic. The Dominican dictator, General Rafael Trujillo, ordered a purge (removal) of all the Haitians living in the Dominican Republic. Some 15,000 Haitians were murdered by Trujillo's soldiers. This action widened the rift that already existed between Haitians and Dominicans. That rift still exists today.

In 1946, the Haitian military took control of the government. It placed Dumarsais Estimé in power. It had been more than thirty years since there had been a black president in Haiti. Estimé's rule, known as the Black

Revolution, brought a temporary end to mulatto dominance in Haiti. But increased poverty and hunger led to Estimé's overthrow, by the same army that had placed him in power.

Paul Magloire, an army officer, became president in December 1950. He worked to improve living conditions for Haitians, but he governed as a dictator. At the end of his term, in 1956, Magloire refused to leave office. But like many Haitian presidents before him, he was ousted by a military coup.

Haiti was left in a state of chaos. And again, Haitians wondered if there was any leader who could rule the country with stability. The answer to their question was about to be answered.

Paul Magloire replaced Dumarsais Estimé as Haiti's president in 1950. He spent six years in office before being overthrown by the military.

Chapter 3

The Long Dictatorship

For most of 1957, the nation of Haiti remained in a state of complete political chaos. The government experienced a cycle of provisional (temporary) presidents and military overthrows. Finally, in September of that year, the army organized new elections. There were four candidates for president. The army then, however, allowed only one candidate—François Duvalier—to conduct a campaign. To no one's surprise, Duvalier was elected president.

The Doctor in Charge

François Duvalier, who was affectionately nicknamed "Papa Doc," was a popular black country doctor in Haiti. Duvalier first became known there for his work fighting malaria and other diseases. A man with political ambitions, Duvalier had served in the cabinet of Dumarsais Estimé during the Black Revolution. As Haiti's new president, Papa Doc dubbed himself "Leader of the Blacks." He told the impoverished peasants that he was the key to their survival and growth.

Duvalier quickly established himself as a dictator. He did not allow anyone to criticize him. He closed down

The Duvaliers—
Papa Doc
and then Baby
Doc—ruled
Haiti for nearly
thirty years.

Opposite:
François Duvalier (standing) and his son Jean-Claude Duvalier (seated), in a campaign poster to promote Jean-Claude to the Haitian people.

Secret Police: The Tontons Macoute

As Haiti's dictator, François Duvalier organized a secret police force called the *Tontons Macoute*. The name is a Creole voodoo term, often translated as "bogeyman." In Haitian nursery tales, Tonton Macoute is a scary man who comes at Christmas to carry away children who have been bad. He puts them in his *macoute*, a straw shoulder bag worn by Haitian peasants. The word *tonton* means "uncle" in French and Creole.

During his reign, François ("Papa Doc") Duvalier employed some 10,000 Tontons Macoute. He recruited them mostly from Haiti's slums and countryside. Their uniform usually consisted of blue jeans, denim hats, sunglasses, red bandannas—and pistols. The job of the Tontons Macoute was to beat, jail, and sometimes kill individuals considered enemies of the government. While the Tontons Macoute operated, up to 60,000 Haitians were murdered.

At first, Papa Doc called the Tontons Macoute the Civilian Militia. Later, they became known officially as the Volunteers of National Security (VNS). (Not all VNS members were Tonton Macoutes.) With over 10,000 members, the Tontons Macoute outnumbered the Haitian army 2 to 1.

Duvalier was careful to make sure that the Tontons Macoute did not get out of his control. To balance their power, he also assigned some terrorist activities to members of Haiti's regular army and police force. He made sure that the army officers did not become too powerful, either. At one point, Papa Doc closed Haiti's Military Academy, where top officers were trained. He also had an important colonel assassinated. This helped to ensure that Duvalier would not be toppled by the military, as had happened to many Haitian presidents in the past.

Of all Duvalier's enforcers, the Tontons Macoute were the most feared. They spied on citizens, imposed censorship, and were violent. They were known for their torture, imprisonment without trial, and exile of political opponents.

Even after François Duvalier's death in 1971, the Tontons Macoute continued to operate in Haiti, though not as openly as in the past. During the reign of Jean-Claude Duvalier, many Haitians felt it was not always clear whether the president controlled the Tontons Macoute or vice versa. After Jean-Claude's departure, many Tontons Macoute went into exile.

Art is an important part of Haitian culture and provides a way for people to express themselves. In this painting, both children and adults chase the Tontons Macoute out of their neighborhood.

Papa Doc, dressed in his characteristic black clothes, used fear and intimidation to control the Haitian people.

newspapers, as well as radio and television stations, that said anything negative about either him or his family. Duvalier also organized a secret police force known as the Tontons Macoute. Members were given the power to attack, imprison, and kill individuals opposed to Duvalier policies. As a result of the terror, thousands of Haitians began to go into exile.

To control the Haitian masses, Duvalier also used psychology. Papa Doc was well aware of the people's strong belief in voodoo, and he used it to his advantage. For example, he changed the colors of the national flag from blue and red to black and red—the colors of secret voodoo societies. (Today, the flag is again blue and red.)

Duvalier wanted Haitians to believe that he himself was a voodoo spirit. In voodoo tradition, the spirit of death dresses in black. Therefore, Duvalier always made sure to wear black—a black suit, black hat, and dark sunglasses.

Many Haitians indeed thought that Duvalier was Baron Samedi, the spirit of death. Rumors spread that Duvalier slept in a grave and kept the shrunken heads of his enemies in his office. Haitians prayed to him to curse and defeat their enemies. They believed that Papa Doc had secret powers to foretell the future.

Duvalier did take careful measures to control the future. In 1963, he even prepared a new constitution for Haiti that made him president for life. Opponents tried to stop him but failed. Throughout the early 1960s, some Haitians who were in exile made several attempts to invade the island, but they were poorly organized. These exiled Haitians even appealed to the United States, which did cut off all aid to Haiti in 1962 to protest the harsh government repression. Later in the 1960s, however, aid to Haiti was restored. The United States felt that Duvalier had at least one redeeming quality: He wasn't a Communist. (During this time, the United States was concerned about the spread of communism, especially to nearby countries.)

While Duvalier managed to remain in power, he did not at all succeed in improving living conditions for the poor. Government corruption and mismanagement led to sharp economic declines. As a result, Duvalier also alienated many wealthy Haitians. Mulattos began leaving Haiti to live in other countries.

Like Father, Like Son

François Duvalier died in 1971. But before he died, he named his son, Jean-Claude, to succeed him. The Haitian constitution required that the president be at least twenty years old. But Jean-Claude, nicknamed "Baby Doc," was only nineteen. The Haitian legislature resolved this problem simply by declaring that Jean-Claude was, in fact, twenty-one years old. Baby Doc thus became the new leader of Haiti.

Jean-Claude Duvalier generally continued his father's policies. In some ways, however, he tried to be less harsh as a dictator. He ordered the Tontons Macoute to stop terrorizing political enemies, although he continued to use them for personal protection. He also released some political prisoners in an effort to strengthen Haiti's relations with the United States.

Baby Doc established new programs, supposedly to improve the Haitian economy. He received large amounts of foreign aid. But the money generally did not benefit the grossly impoverished Haitian masses. Instead, most went to the ruling elite for deposit into their foreign bank accounts. Jean-Claude Duvalier was criticized for having a luxurious lifestyle, which included owning a yacht, seaside villa, ranch, and mountain hideaway, in addition to his home in the National Palace. His wife, Michel Bennette Duvalier, was also criticized for her lavish spending sprees in Paris and New York.

Meanwhile, the Haitian people continued to suffer. By 1980, as many as 50,000 Haitians a year were fleeing in boats to Florida. In September 1981, the U.S. government tried to stem this seemingly constant flow of Haitian immigrants. President Ronald Reagan said that the Haitians were economic refugees, and not political ones. (Economic refugees are people who are trying to escape severe poverty. Political refugees are people who are fleeing persecution by their government and whose lives may be in danger if they are sent back to their home country.) Under President Reagan's policy, economic refugees were not eligible for asylum in the United States. The U.S. Coast Guard stopped, and returned, nearly all of the Haitian "boat people."

During the early 1980s, protests against Jean-Claude Duvalier increased greatly in Haiti. At one point, Baby Doc jailed one hundred journalists who publicly opposed him. In 1983, Pope John Paul II visited Haiti and urged change so that "the poor of every kind might be able to hope again." Baby Doc banned newspapers from printing the pope's speech.

By 1984, large-scale riots against the government took place. Crowds of hungry Haitians looted food warehouses in many small towns. Roman Catholic priests in Haiti became more vocal in their opposition to Duvalier.

Baby Doc held an election in 1985 to prove that he was still popular. Because Duvalier's government rigged the voting, he got 99 percent of the vote. But protests against Duvalier continued and spread from the small towns to larger Haitian cities.

Following these events, the United States decided to withdraw its support of Duvalier. It claimed that Haiti's ruler did not uphold minimal standards of freedom and

On January 31, 1986, in the presence of one hundred supporters, Jean-Claude Duvalier personally denied the rumor that his regime had fallen. His message was broadcast on Haiti's radio system.

human decency. In February 1986, a U.S. fleet surrounded the harbor at the capital city of Port-au-Prince. Baby Doc knew that his reign was over. He feared that he and his family would be murdered or imprisoned if they stayed in Haiti any longer. On February 6, 1986, in the middle of the night and under heavy guard, Jean-Claude Duvalier left Haiti. He, his family, and some of his aides escaped on a U.S. Air Force plane to France.

A Shaky Rule

The Haitian masses were relieved when the Duvalier father-son regime ended after nearly thirty years. They believed that the country was finally rid of its dictators. Many Haitians who had fled to the United States in the

A group of ecstatic Haitians ride through the streets of Port-au-Prince to celebrate the end of Baby Doc's regime. Duvalier's departure was also marked with riots and looting.

1970s and 1980s decided to return home. They felt that now there was finally a real chance for Haiti to establish a democracy.

The leadership of Haiti was assumed by army commander General Henri Namphy. But his government faced critical problems. The Duvaliers had left little money in the Haitian treasury. In addition, half the workers were unemployed. Most children suffered from malnutrition as well as tuberculosis and other diseases.

Despite these crises, General Namphy began to make progress. He introduced a new constitution, which promised the Haitian people free elections, free speech, jobs, and education. In 1986, Namphy's government dissolved the Haitian National Assembly, which had served merely as a "rubber stamp" for all Duvalier policies. The new constitution called for a National Assembly to be elected by the people. An independent civilian commission would oversee the election.

The hope for democracy in Haiti did not last long, however. On election day, in November 1987, the army prevented the civilian council from functioning. Soldiers and the Tontons Macoute massacred more than thirty voters at the polling places. The elections had to be cancelled.

In January 1988, new elections were held. The voters elected a civilian president, Leslie Manigat, whom the army kept under its control. But Manigat's rule did not last long. In June of that year, General Namphy overthrew the government and once again took charge of Haiti. He then quickly declared himself president of a military government.

However, Namphy's regained rule was also short-lived. After his soldiers attacked a church and killed thirteen parishioners, the army decided to remove Namphy from power. He was succeeded by Lieutenant General Prosper Avril, a former financial adviser to the Duvaliers. Avril declared himself president.

On taking office in 1986, General Namphy promised a "real and working democracy" for Haiti. But, like many Haitian leaders before him, Namphy did not keep his promises.

Avril ruled Haiti as a dictator. During his reign in 1989, more than thirty government opponents were arrested and beaten. In Duvalier fashion, Avril censored the media and suspended parts of the constitution. The Haitian people protested and rebelled. As a result, Avril was forced to resign in March 1990. He then fled to Florida.

Avril's successor was Ertha Pascal-Trouillot, Haiti's first female supreme court justice. She ruled as a provisional president, along with a nineteen-member council of regional representatives of the democratic movement. She agreed to serve as Haiti's leader until new elections could be held.

When Avril resigned in 1990, some Haitians celebrated by looting a government building. Here, one man raises his arms behind a bonfire fueled by the items taken from the building.

Chapter 4

Crisis at Home and Abroad

In 1990, Father Jean-Bertrand Aristide was a popular, thirty-six-year-old Roman Catholic priest who had been an outspoken advocate of equality and democracy in Haiti. He had protested loudly against the evil and corruption that plagued Haiti's government. Gaining large support from Haiti's poor blacks, Aristide decided to run for president in the 1990 elections. His political party was called *Lavalas*, Creole for "Rushing Waters." His campaign slogan was "Take Haiti from misery to poverty, with dignity."

A Change in Leadership

The 1990 election of Aristide was a historic moment in Haitian history. For the first time ever, the country held free elections—the military was not in charge of the process. The promise for real democracy in Haiti finally was at hand.

As president, Aristide attempted to enact major reforms. These included fixing mismanagement of public administration and an end to military corruption. Since the early 1980s, the Haitian military had been involved in trafficking millions of dollars worth of cocaine through Haiti to

Hopes for democracy are dashed as Haiti enters a new reign of terror.

Opposite:
Haiti had a renewed hope for democracy with the first-ever free elections and the people's candidate, Jean-Bertrand Aristide.

the United States. Immediately after taking office, President Aristide announced that he was retiring Haiti's top military officers.

The new president also wished to aid Haiti's poor blacks, who had been ignored by virtually all previous leaders. The day after taking office, Aristide welcomed the poor onto the lawn of the National Palace for a free meal. He helped serve the people himself. Aristide announced plans to give farmers more land and to increase workers' minimum wage.

But Aristide's programs were met with strong opposition. His efforts for reform, which included taxing the rich, did not please the Haitian upper classes.

Raoul Cédras led a coup that overthrew Aristide in 1991 and marked the beginning of a new dictatorship in Haiti.

Aristide also alienated the military with his plans to end corruption and drug trafficking. Army officers soon began plotting Aristide's overthrow, which took place on September 29, 1991, only nine months after he took office. The coup was led by Lieutenant General Raoul Cédras, whom Aristide had appointed chief of staff. Cédras was aided by police commander Colonel Michel François and army chief of staff General Philippe Biamby. With Cédras in charge, Aristide fled in exile to the United States.

Cédras's seizure of power marked the start of a new reign of terror in Haiti. Haitians who favored Aristide's return were beaten, jailed, and worse. Lavalas members who either organized or attended pro-democracy rallies frequently were attacked. Violence was carried out by soldiers, the police, and armed civilian enforcers called "attachés." In reality, the attachés were merely a new version of the Tontons Macoute who had served under the Duvaliers years earlier. (Although some of the Tontons Macoute had fled after Baby Doc's departure, many had remained. Those who had remained had continued to exert force when they felt it was necessary. The members of the Tontons Macoute who had gone into exile returned to Haiti after the overthrow of President Jean-Bertrand Aristide.)

Violence and terror reigned. In poor neighborhoods, Haitian men frequently were questioned and beaten by soldiers and police, and women often were raped. Soldiers traveled to Haiti's mountains to hunt down people who supported Aristide. They burned crops and killed animals, stopping farmers from growing food or making a living. In all, more than 3,000 Aristide supporters were killed in the three years following the 1991 military coup.

Starting in 1993, much torture was carried out by a new civilian group called the Front for the Advancement and Progress of Haiti (FRAPH, which sounds like the French word for "beat.") The group was formed by Emmanuel Constant, a man seeking to become Haiti's new president.

The Many Sides of Aristide

Aristide became a controversial figure, by simultaneously promoting democracy and political violence.

After being deposed as Haitian president in September 1991, Father Jean-Bertrand Aristide fled to Washington, D.C., where he lived in political exile. Many Haitians and Americans supported the Roman Catholic priest's return to power. Yet others found him to be a puzzling individual, unclear and sometimes contradictory in his political intentions.

Did President Aristide favor a U.S. invasion of Haiti in order to remove coup leader Cédras? In January 1994, Aristide said that he would "support a surgical strike by an international force" in Haiti. But in June 1994, he said, "Never, never, never would I agree to be restored to power by an invasion." He explained that Haiti's constitution forbids support of foreign military intervention. Yet a month later, he asked the United Nations (UN) to take "swift and definitive action" against those who had ousted him.

Many Americans accused Aristide of wanting it both ways—wanting the United States to fight for his return, but being able to condemn the U.S.

action afterward. Robert White, a retired American diplomat, said, "He doesn't want to give a total green light to the United States to occupy Haiti. Once he is back, he wants to be able to say, 'I enjoy popular support and don't require your long-term presence here.'"

Critics also questioned what Aristide might do if returned to power. Would he take revenge on his opponents in Haiti? In exile, Aristide had often said, "We seek reconciliation, not vengeance." Yet shortly before his overthrow, he gave a speech in Port-au-Prince that indicated otherwise. Aristide told supporters to give the enemy "what he deserves." He praised the practice of "Pére Lebrun," or necklacing—placing a tire over a victim's shoulders and setting it on fire. In a March 1994 *Current History* report, Aristide called Pére Lebrun "a beautiful instrument" with a "good smell."

While Cédras continued his reign, Aristide remained Haiti's best hope for democracy. Yet many people—both in Haiti and in the United States—remained concerned about his intentions.

FRAPH was accused of committing more than one hundred political executions during its first year of operation. One of its most violent acts took place in December 1993. FRAPH terrorists raided Cité Soleil, Port-au-Prince's largest slum and the home of many Aristide supporters, and burned hundreds of shacks to the ground, killing some residents.

Following the overthrow of Aristide, thousands of his supporters were killed by military attachés. The streets of Haiti were marked by destruction.

UN Action

Haiti's reign of terror did not go unnoticed by the rest of the world. The United States was concerned with human rights abuses there. It was also worried about how a dictatorship in Haiti might affect neighboring countries. President George Bush worked to secure UN economic sanctions against Haiti. The intention was to place economic pressure on the Haitian government, thus forcing Cédras to step down. Then President Aristide could return to restore democracy in Haiti.

In November 1991, sanctions were declared by the Organization of American States (OAS)—a UN group that includes several Latin American countries and the United States. The OAS enacted a trade embargo, which banned all shipments of arms and oil to Haiti. In May 1992, OAS trade restrictions were increased. In June 1993, a new UN embargo also went into effect. However, these sanctions did not hurt the ruling military as much as they hurt Haiti's poor. People now had even more difficulty getting food, medicine, and other basic needs. All the while, Cédras refused to step down.

A Broken Promise

By July 1993, it appeared that sanctions against Haiti might have finally worked. That month, Cédras signed a formal agreement in New York to give back control of the Haitian government to President Aristide by October 30, 1993. The agreement called for a new cabinet, to be chosen by Aristide. Also, an international military group would help supervise Haiti's police and army.

In August 1993, Robert Malval was sworn in as premier of Haiti in Aristide's cabinet. In that same month, the United Nations ended its sanctions against Haiti.

It soon became clear, however, that Cédras did not intend to honor the agreement. The Haitian military continued to use violence against Aristide supporters. Victims were not just the poor, either. On September 11, 1993, gunmen killed a wealthy businessman and Aristide supporter named Antoine Izmery. They dragged Izmery from church and shot him in the street. A month later, on October 14, Haitian Justice Minister Guy Malary was also murdered in broad daylight. Malary had been working to reform Haiti's corrupt justice system.

One of Cédras's most defiant actions occurred on October 11, 1993. On that day, the American troop ship *Harlan County* approached the dock at Port-au-Prince. It carried 218 American and Canadian soldiers and engineers. They had come to help train a new Haitian army and police force, in accordance with the July 1993 agreement. But instead of being welcomed, the envoy was challenged at the docks by an angry crowd of Cédras supporters. Several hundred protesters waved guns and

Marronage: Haitians in Hiding

In the three years following the 1991 military coup, some 50,000 refugees fled Haiti in boats. But more Haitians were unable—or unwilling—to leave their homeland. Instead, they began living in *marronage*, Creole for "hiding." In essence, they went into exile in their own country.

By mid-1994, it was estimated that 100,000 to 300,000 Haitians were hiding from soldiers and attachés (armed civilian enforcers). Many fled to Haiti's mountains, where they remained separated from their families, sometimes for years. Others moved outside their villages, into the brush. They returned home each morning, after army patrols left, to collect food and money. Men often wore disguises, dressing as merchant women to move about their villages safely.

Marronage is not a new phenomenon in Haiti. It dates back to the 1600s, when black slaves in the French colony began escaping from the plantations. They fled to the Haitian mountains.

In the current crisis, those living in marronage have included important political figures. In September 1993, attachés shot up the office of Evans Paul, the mayor of Port-au-Prince. Paul began sleeping in a different house every night and using several different offices each week. After being removed as Haiti's premier in May 1994, Robert Malval remained mostly in his hillside villa, hidden behind high stone walls. He left only occasionally to visit diplomats, in a bulletproof car provided by the United States.

No one doubted that marronage was a dangerous existence. But for many Haitians, it was the only answer until democracy could be restored to their country. As one Haitian put it, "You learn to live like a bat. You fly at night."

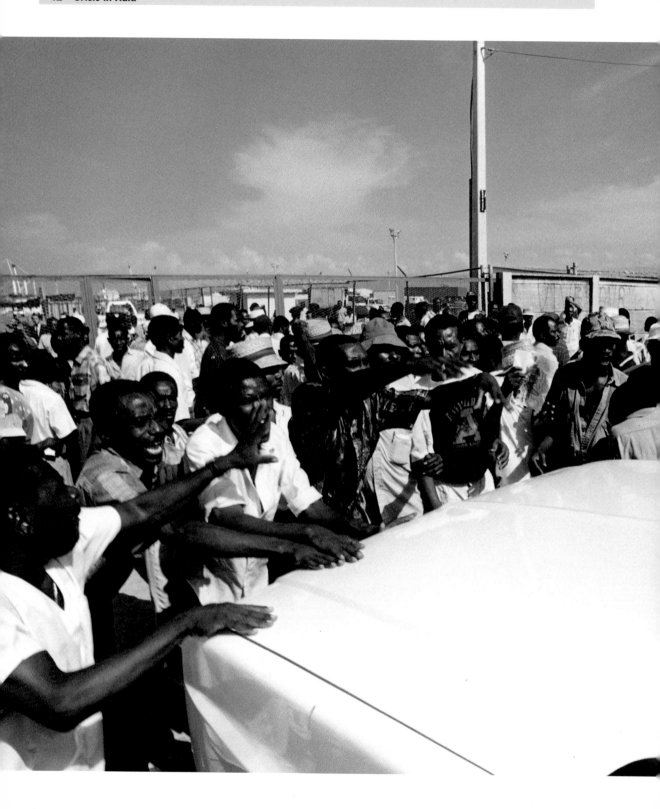

knives at the ship and shouted anti-American slogans. They also attacked a car carrying U.S. diplomats.

The next day, President Bill Clinton ordered the *Harlan County* to leave Haiti. Clinton said that the retreat was to ensure the safety of the passengers on board. However, people in Haiti and abroad saw the withdrawal as a great embarrassment for the United States. Cédras supporters celebrated their success in keeping foreigners from interfering in Haiti's affairs.

More Sanctions and Embargoes

In response to Cédras's actions, the UN Security Council voted in October 1993, to place sanctions on Haiti again, and they banned the delivery of oil to the country. The effect was felt immediately. By November, many Haitian schools and businesses had closed due to an oil shortage. Most public transportation and garbage collection had also ceased.

As before, critics argued that the embargo was unfair because it mainly hurt the Haitian poor. In November 1993, it was reported that 1,000 children a month were dying in Haiti due to a lack of food deliveries. Defending the embargo, William Gray, President Clinton's envoy (representative) to Haiti said, "Do sanctions hurt? Yes, they do. But dictatorships kill."

Despite the restrictions, the Cédras dictatorship continued. So, in May 1994, the United Nations increased its economic sanctions against Haiti. Now the delivery of all items, except food and medicine, was banned. Haitian smugglers, however, found ways to sneak gas and other supplies into the country through its neighbor, the Dominican Republic. President Clinton then sought an increase in supervision along the border of the Dominican Republic. In August 1994, the president of the Dominican Republic, Joaquín Balaguer, promised that the border with Haiti would be sealed.

Opposite:
A mob of angry, pro-Cédras Haitians attacks a U.S. embassy car in front of the entrance to Port-au-Prince harbor on October 11, 1993, in response to the arrival of the *Harlan County*.

In addition to the UN bans, the United States took its own measures against Haiti. In January 1994, President Clinton froze the visas and U.S. bank accounts of all Haitian military officers. Later, he extended the freeze to all Haitian citizens. This meant that Haitians could not wire money from U.S. accounts to Haiti or make new deposits in American banks. In addition, Clinton blocked all U.S. money transactions with businesses connected to the Haitian military.

Economic sanctions imposed on Haiti took a dramatic toll on the lives of Haiti's poor. These children, photographed in June 1994, suffer from severe lack of nutrition.

By August 1994, the UN and U.S. sanctions against Haiti had taken greater hold. With no goods being either exported or imported, the Haitian economy was extremely weak. More and more businesses had been forced to close down. Half of all Haitian workers were unemployed and many homes had no electricity or food. CARE (Cooperative for American Relief Everywhere) and other relief organizations were feeding more than one million Haitians a day.

Haitians both rich and poor were affected by the sanctions. Without gasoline for cars, even the wealthiest citizens were restricted in their ability to travel. By August 1994, all commercial air service in and out of Haiti had been suspended. In effect, Haitians were trapped in their own country.

Dictatorship Continues

Despite rising pressures, Cédras refused to allow President Aristide to return to power. On May 11, 1994, Cédras had tried to give his government more credibility by naming Émile Jonassaint as provisional president. President Clinton called the installation of Jonassaint illegal. In Haiti, Premier Malval asked government workers to disobey orders from Jonassaint and the military. In response, Jonassaint removed Malval from office five days later. Jonassaint declared that he would serve both as president and premier of Haiti.

During the summer of 1994, the possibility of a U.S. invasion of Haiti grew much stronger. In August 1994, Jonassaint declared a state of siege in Haiti. This allowed the government to formally suspend constitutional rights and give more power to the military. It officially became illegal for Haitians to speak in favor of an American invasion. But as one Haitian businessman said, "We've already been living under a state of siege for nearly three years. This declaration merely formalizes an ugly reality."

Chapter 5

What Can Be Done?

As the crisis in Haiti worsened in 1994, international concern grew deeper. Americans debated what should be done about the thousands of Haitian refugees who sought a haven in the United States. Foreign governments discussed how much they should get involved in the politics of Haiti. And Haitians themselves argued about the best way to bring peace and stability to their homeland.

A Wavering Refugee Policy

The U.S. policy toward Haitian refugees changed many times in the early 1990s. In May 1992, President George Bush ordered that all Haitian refugees be returned home without having asylum hearings—interviews that would determine their refugee status. Bill Clinton, running for president in 1992, attacked that policy as illegal and immoral. Yet after he was elected, Clinton feared that more Haitians would come to the United States. In January 1993, he announced that he would temporarily continue the Bush policy.

In May 1994, as reports of human rights abuses in Haiti grew, Clinton changed his policy. He declared that all Haitian refugees would be given asylum hearings aboard

Together, the United States and the United Nations find a solution to the crisis in Haiti.

Opposite:
Haitian refugees take cover under a tarp on board a U.S. Coast Guard ship docked at Guantánamo Bay naval base in order to handle the overflow of people.

U.S. ships in the Caribbean Sea. Only those Haitians who were judged to be political refugees would be given asylum in the United States. Haitians deemed economic refugees would not. President Clinton's announcement served to set off a whole new flood of Haitians fleeing their country.

During June and July 1994, some 20,000 Haitian refugees attempted to reach Miami, Florida. The U.S. naval base at Guantánamo Bay, Cuba, overflowed with 16,500 refugees. On July 6, President Clinton changed

In July 1994, Guantánamo Bay naval base in Cuba was filled with thousands of refugees seeking asylum.

his policy once again. He declared that Haitian refugees who were picked up at sea would be offered safe haven—but not in the United States. Clinton also said that only those Haitians who applied within Haiti for asylum would be eligible to enter the United States.

International Involvement

To carry out his refugee plan, President Clinton needed the cooperation of many foreign governments. Their response was mixed. In July 1994, the president of Panama, Guillermo Endara, said that his country would accept up to 10,000 Haitian refugees for a year. But only a few days later, Endara went back on his promise. Panama already suffered from a housing shortage, a rising crime rate, and serious health and drug crises. Many Panamanians feared that things would only worsen if thousands of refugees were suddenly taken in.

Other countries in the region reluctantly agreed to help out. Grenada, for example, agreed "in principle" to take in some of the Haitian refugees. Suriname, St. Lucia, Turks & Caicos, and Barbuda also offered safe havens. Honduras offered temporary refuge for up to 40,000 Haitians, in return for foreign aid. The small islands of Dominica and Antigua each agreed to take 2,000 refugees. President Clinton also sought the help of countries outside the Caribbean area, including Canada, Australia, and Great Britain.

But accepting refugees was not the only global involvement sought by the United States. President Clinton asked the United Nations to approve and participate in a possible invasion of Haiti. The United States requested that France, Canada, Venezuela, and other countries form a multinational force. This force would maintain peace in Haiti after Americans led the invasion. Several Latin American and Caribbean governments agreed to send peacekeeping troops to Haiti, on one condition—that UN

In July 1994, U.S. Marines boarded the U.S.S. *Portland* and sailed toward Haiti after the UN Security Council approved an American-led invasion of the island nation.

sanctions, not U.S. guns—force out Cédras. These governments bitterly remembered American invasions of their own countries in the past.

In July 1994, the UN Security Council approved an American-led invasion of Haiti. It passed a resolution authorizing the use of "all necessary means" to remove Cédras from power. U.S. Marines were deployed to waters off of Haiti.

But by August 1994, many Latin American countries were having doubts about the effectiveness of an invasion. Brazil, Chile, Colombia, Ecuador, and Peru all refused to send any military units. Brazil's president, Itamar Franco, said, "The defense of democracy should not rely on the use of coercive measures, with unpredictable results."

Doing the Right Thing?

President Clinton now had UN approval to invade Haiti. But in the United States, as elsewhere, people debated whether an invasion was the best course of action. The issue divided the American public, members of Congress, and even officials within the Clinton administration.

Those favoring an invasion argued that it was the only way left to get rid of Cédras. Three years of sanctions and embargoes had simply not worked. The United States had a moral obligation to end the terror in Haiti as soon as possible. Current sanctions were not working fast enough, they claimed. Meanwhile, the U.S. naval base at Guantánamo Bay was poorly equipped to hold refugees any longer. Haitians there had no work, recreational activities, or reading materials. The sooner an invasion, the sooner the refugees could return home.

Some Americans felt that *not* invading Haiti smacked of racism. After all, the United States had invaded other Caribbean countries in recent years, including Panama and Grenada. If the United States didn't go into Haiti, critics charged, it would be because Haitians are largely black. Were they white, they said, the United States would have already moved in to help.

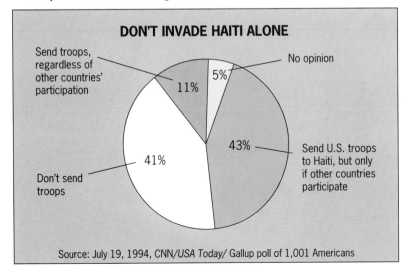

DON'T INVADE HAITI ALONE

Send troops, regardless of other countries' participation — 11%

No opinion — 5%

Send U.S. troops to Haiti, but only if other countries participate — 43%

Don't send troops — 41%

Source: July 19, 1994, CNN/USA Today/ Gallup poll of 1,001 Americans

President Clinton said that he considered an invasion of Haiti because "it's in our backyard." Many Americans shared his concern: Chaos in Haiti could lead to chaos in neighboring countries, including the Dominican Republic and Cuba. That might mean even more refugees fleeing to the United States in the future.

People opposed to an invasion also had their reasons. They claimed that the United States had no vital interests in Haiti. Risking soldiers' lives there was thus not justified. Besides, they said, democracy and human rights never existed in Haiti before. Restoring Aristide wouldn't guarantee their future existence. After all, the invasion of U.S. Marines in 1915 did not change politics in Haiti, even after nineteen years of American occupation.

Americans were not united in their opinions about what action the United States should take against Cédras. Here, demonstrators in New York City protest U.S. intervention.

A Dictator's Defiance

"I am the pin in Haiti's hand grenade. If pulled, an explosion will occur." These are the words of Lieutenant General Raoul Cédras, Haiti's army chief, who seized control of the government in 1991. For three years, Cédras refused to step down and allow President Jean-Bertrand Aristide to return to power. As the threat of an American invasion grew in the summer of 1994, so did Cédras's acts of defiance.

In July 1994, Cédras ordered out of Haiti nearly one hundred human-rights observers from the United Nations and the OAS (Organization of American States). He gave them only forty-eight hours to vacate the country. At the airport, army officers harassed these human-rights monitors before they left. Luggage was inspected and shots were fired, though no one was hurt. After the group was expelled, soldiers dumped the bodies of a dozen murdered peasants on a Haitian village street. Local residents were ordered to bury the dead.

In July, Cédras also struck out at Haitians who were trying to flee the country. Describing their mass exodus as a "political action," he ordered troops to shoot at refugees sailing from Haiti's shores. Soldiers burned boats being prepared for future refugees. In August 1994, police in Port-au-Prince attacked a crowd of Haitians who stood in line to apply for refuge in the United States. Applicants were forced to lie on the ground and then were beaten with batons. Also in August 1994, the Reverend Jean-Marie Vincent, a well-known supporter of Aristide, was shot and killed by attachés.

Lieutenant General Cédras made it clear that he would not restore President Aristide to power. In August 1994, he announced plans to put Aristide on trial for treason. His crime, Cédras claimed, was asking the United Nations to take "swift and decisive action." Cédras also declared a state of siege in Haiti. Haitian soldiers and civilians marched in public drills, preparing for a possible attack by the United States.

Raoul Cédras showed no sign of weakening even when the United Nations became involved with the plight of Haiti and approved an invasion.

At that point, no one was sure if, or when, an American invasion might take place. Cédras continued to insist that he would not back away from U.S. and UN threats and that he was not going to give up quietly.

People also argued that after invading, the United States would be burdened with keeping law and order in a lawless country. Marines would be attacked by soldiers and attachés. Cédras supporters had already threatened to poison water supplies. Unable to speak Creole, U.S. Marines would be in danger in a foreign land.

Many Americans feared that once there, the United States would never be able to withdraw quickly. The job of building up Haiti would require 20,000 U.S. soldiers and billions of dollars in U.S. aid—for years to come. As one military source said, "The minute the first U.S. soldier lands, you're responsible for everything that happens in the country."

A Decision Is Made

By September 1994, the Clinton administration felt that Cédras had to be removed immediately. Haiti's food and fuel crisis had grown much worse. Terrorism against Haitians continued, including the murder on August 28 of Roman Catholic priest Jean-Marie Vincent. Dozens of Aristide supporters, as well as orphaned children, were being murdered in the streets each week. In addition, the situation at Guantánamo Bay had badly deteriorated. Haitians detained there were rioting and fighting with U.S. military police, complaining of a lack of clean clothes and running water.

President Clinton decided he could wait no longer for UN sanctions to pressure Cédras into leaving. On September 15, in a televised address, Clinton warned Haiti's leaders: "Your time is up. Leave now or we will force you from power." In a final effort to avoid a military confrontation, Clinton sent a three-member negotiation team to Haiti the following day. Former U.S. president Jimmy Carter, retired army general Colin Powell, and Senator Sam Nunn spent two days trying to work out an agreement with Cédras. To the relief of the U. S. government

and others, the delegation's efforts were successful—in the nick of time. As U.S. planes began their journey to Haiti to invade, Cédras agreed to give up power by October 15, paving the way for Aristide's return as Haiti's president.

On September 19, 1994, some 3,000 American troops landed in Haiti on what had changed overnight from an invasion to a peacekeeping mission. The forces met no resistance and quickly took control of airfields and ports at Port-au-Prince and Cap-Haitien.

The vast majority of Haitian citizens celebrated the American presence in their country. Aristide supporters filled the streets to welcome the troops. But their mood did not remain cheerful for long. On the second day of American occupation, Haitian police, soldiers, and

American troops that landed in Haiti on a peacekeeping mission in September 1994, were greeted by relieved Haitian citizens.

attachés were back on the streets. They beat Aristide supporters attending a pro-democracy rally in Port-au-Prince, killing at least one participant. American troops were under orders not to intervene, and could only watch the violence in frustration without taking action.

But as attacks on Haitians increased in the coming days, American troops—now totalling about 9,000—were given instructions to step in. They actively stopped Haitian police from beating citizens. As a result, the number of street attacks decreased, but violence did not end entirely. On September 24, American Marines shot ten members of the Haitian police who had fired at U.S. troops. The next day, Marines began dismantling the Haitian military's supply of guns and ammunition.

In late September 1994, Haitian citizens voluntarily joined in disarming the Haitian military and turned over hundreds of weapons to U.S. troops.

Aristide supporters returned to their celebratory mood. But in some cities and towns, celebration turned into chaos. On September 25, hundreds of Haitian civilians in Cap-Haitien looted police buildings and seized rifles. Ironically, Marines now found themselves having to protect Haitian military members from attacks by civilians. Marines tried to control the situation, and appealed to Haitian citizens to return the stolen weapons. Over the next several days, Haitians turned in more than 200 guns taken from police stations. But trouble remained. Haitians continued to loot food warehouses, and mobs frequently beat Haitian army members and sympathizers.

By the end of September, more than 20,000 American troops were stationed in Haiti. Nevertheless, violence on both sides continued. On September 29, five Haitians were killed after a bomb was tossed into a crowd attending a pro-democracy rally in Port-au-Prince. The next day, attachés from FRAPH shot and killed eight more Aristide supporters in the capital city. U.S. troops had been stationed away from the shootings, trying to protect food stores and warehouses because Haitian looters had taken some eleven tons of food from aid-agency warehouses.

In October, American troops increased their search for Haitian military arms. U.S. soldiers invaded FRAPH headquarters in Port-au-Prince and detained more than a dozen attachés inside, including the personal bodyguards of Cédras. They also searched other buildings and homes and confiscated military weapons.

As the October 15 deadline for the departure of Cédras neared, Haiti's civilian leaders slowly began to reappear. Evans Paul, mayor of Port-au-Prince, returned to his City Hall offices after being forced to conduct political activities in secrecy for more than a year. At the same time, some of Haiti's key military personnel began to leave. On October 4, Colonel Michel François, the police chief of Port-au-Prince, fled to go to the Dominican Republic. One of François's main allies, FRAPH leader Emmanuel

Constant, announced that he no longer opposed the return of Aristide to Haiti.

Finally, the three-year military rule in Haiti officially came to an end. Nearly a week earlier than expected, on October 10, Cédras resigned as commander in chief of the Haitian armed forces. In a brief ceremony, he told Haitian soldiers, "I choose to leave our country for your protection, so that my presence will not be a motive for actions against the military establishment or a pretext for unjustified actions." Cédras's top aide, General Philippe Biamby, also resigned.

The Future of Haiti

On October 15, 1994, President Aristide returned to Haiti in triumph. A huge crowd of joyous supporters turned out to greet him at the National Palace in Port-au-Prince. Throwing a dove of peace into the air, Aristide told the people, "Honor, respect." Then he added, "No to violence, no to vengeance, yes to reconciliation." It had been more than three years since his forced exile from his homeland. Now, thanks to intervention by the United States and other nations, Aristide was free to complete his term as Haiti's first democratically-elected leader.

The future of Haiti was still unclear. Years of dictatorship and human rights abuses had taken a harsh toll, weakening both the economy and the people's spirit. Nevertheless, Haiti still had a unique legacy upon which to build. It was once the richest territory in the Western Hemisphere, and it was the first black-led republic in the world. Haitians have preserved their cultural traditions for hundreds of years. They remain a proud people, hopeful that they can create a better future for themselves and their families.

Chronology

December 8, 1492 — Christopher Columbus lands on the island of Hayti, later renamed Hispaniola.

1697 — Spain cedes the western third of Hispaniola to France, which renames the territory St. Domingue. Spain retains the eastern two thirds of the island.

1791 — The slaves of St. Domingue rebel against their French masters. France declares the slaves free in 1794.

1799-1803 — France temporarily regains control of St. Domingue. Toussaint L'Ouverture is imprisoned in France and dies in 1803. France surrenders after its soldiers contract yellow fever.

January 1, 1804 — General Jean-Jacques Dessalines declares St. Domingue an independent country, renaming it Haiti. It is the first black republic in the world. Dessalines is assassinated in 1806.

1808-1818 — Haiti is sectioned into two parts. In the north, Henri Christophe rules the blacks. In the south, Alexandre Pétion rules the mulattos.

1818 — Jean-Pierre Boyer reunites Haiti and serves as president until 1843.

1844-1914 — Haiti has thirty-two different rulers over seventy years.

1915 — U.S. Marines invade Haiti. They occupy the country for nineteen years.

1946-1956 — The Haitian military takes control. They place in power and later remove first Dumarsais Estimé and then Paul Magloire.

1957 — François ("Papa Doc") Duvalier becomes president of Haiti. His secret police, the Tontons Macoute, brutally suppress all political opponents.

1971 — François Duvalier dies and is succeeded by his son, Jean-Claude ("Baby Doc") Duvalier.

1986 — Jean-Claude Duvalier and his family escape Haiti aboard a U.S. Air Force plane and fly to France. General Henri Namphy takes charge of the country.

1987 — Free elections in Haiti are disrupted by the Tontons Macoute. More than thirty voters are massacred.

1988 — Leslie Manigat is elected president in January but is overthrown in June by Namphy, who is overthrown in turn in September. Prosper Avril declares himself president.

March 1990	Prosper Avril is forced to resign and flees to Florida.
December 1990	Father Jean-Bertrand Aristide is chosen president of Haiti in the country's first free elections.
September 1991	Jean-Bertrand Aristide is overthrown in a military coup led by Lieutenant General Raoul Cédras. Aristide goes into exile in Washington, D.C.
November 1991	The OAS (Organization of American States) places an embargo on Haiti, banning shipments of arms and oil.
May 1992	U.S. President George Bush orders all Haitian "boat people" returned to Haiti. The OAS imposes new sanctions against Haiti.
June 1993	UN sanctions against Haiti are imposed.
July 1993	Jean-Bertrand Aristide and Raoul Cédras sign an accord in New York. Cédras agrees to turn over power to Aristide by October 30, 1993.
August 1993	Robert Malval is sworn in as Haiti's premier. UN sanctions are lifted.
September 1993	Aristide supporter Antoine Izmery is murdered.
October 1993	Haitian Justice Minister Guy Malary is murdered. The U.S.S. *Harlan County* is ordered to leave Haiti after Cédras supporters protest its arrival at Port-au-Prince. The United Nations reimposes its sanctions on Haiti.
May 1994	Raoul Cédras names Émile Jonassaint as provisional president of Haiti. Premier Robert Malval is removed from office. The United Nations increases its sanctions against Haiti.
July 1994	The United Nations approves a U.S.-led invasion of Haiti.
August 1994	All commercial traffic in and out of Haiti is ended. A state of siege is declared in Haiti.
September 1994	Cédras agrees to step down from power. American troops arrive in Haiti on a peacekeeping mission.
October 1994	Cedras steps down and leaves Haiti to live in Panama. Aristide returns to be reinstated as president.

For Further Reading

Anthony, Suzanne. *Haiti*. New York: Chelsea House, 1989.

Aristide, Jean-Bertrand, with Wargny, Christophe. *Aristide: An Autobiography*. Maryknoll, NY: Orbis Books, 1993.

Condit, Erin. *François and Jean-Claude Duvalier*. New York: Chelsea House, 1989.

Griffiths, John. *Take a Trip to Haiti*. New York: Franklin Watts, 1989.

Hanmer, Trudy J. *Haiti*. New York: Franklin Watts, 1988.

Hoobler, Dorothy and Hoobler, Thomas. *Toussaint L'Ouverture*. New York: Chelsea House, 1990.

Weddle, Ken. *Haiti in Pictures*. Minneapolis, MN: Lerner, 1987.

Index

Acknowledgments and photo credits

Cover and page 8: ©Ron Haviv/SABA; p. 4: U.S. Coast Guard/ Gamma Liaison; pp. 10, 11, 23, 24, 27, 32, 50, 53: AP/Wide World Photos; pp. 12, 46, 48: Wide World Photos, Inc.; pp. 14, 18, 19: North Wind Picture Archives; p. 17: Bettmann; p. 21: UPI/ Bettmann; p. 26: ©Halebian/Liaison; pp. 30, 31: Gamma Liaison; pp. 33, 42: Reuters/Bettmann; p. 34: ©Cynthia Johnson/Gamma Liaison; p. 36: ©Shepard Sherbell/SABA; pp. 38, 39: ©Steve Starr/ SABA; p. 44: ©Alyx Kellington/Gamma Liaison; p. 52: ©Najlah Feanny/SABA; p. 55: ©Alain Buu/Gamma Liaison; p. 56: ©Steve Lehman/SABA.

Map and chart by Madeline Parker/Blackbirch Graphics, Inc.